"Do You Want Haniel
To Get Well?"

"Wilt Thou be Made Whole?"

By Darrell Davis

A Preacher's Look at Biblical Healing

Copyright Page

Simply This Publishing

Kindle Direct Publishing

Cover Painting by Allen Butt

John 5:1-9

A Man Healed at the Pool of Bethesda

1 After this there was a feast of the Jews, and Jesus went up to Jerusalem.

2 Now there is in Jerusalem by the Sheep Gate a pool, which is called in Hebrew, Bethesda, having five porches.

3 In these lay a great multitude of sick people, blind, lame, paralyzed, waiting for the moving of the water.

4 For an angel went down at a certain time into the pool and stirred up the water; then whoever stepped in first, after the stirring of the water, was made well of whatever disease he had.

5 Now a certain man was there who had an infirmity thirty-eight years.

6 When Jesus saw him lying there, and knew that he already had been in that condition a long time, He said to him, "Do you want to be made well?"

7 The sick man answered Him, "Sir, I have no man to put me into the pool when the water is

stirred up; but while I am coming, another steps down before me."

8 Jesus said to him, "Rise, take up your bed and walk."

9 And immediately the man was made well, took up his bed, and walked.

And that day was the Sabbath.

Author's Note: The manuscript for this book was written between 1988 - 1990, and the cover painting was done in 1992 by Allen Butt, just for this book. For almost thirty years this work was never published until 2021. With the exception of correcting grammar errors, dedication, introduction, and back-cover comments, this work remains the same.

DEDICATION

My father had a stroke on November 1982, sometime before 2:00am, and was taken to a hospital. I received a call at 2:30am, and went to prayer. Sometime around 4:00am, I heard The Lord say, *"Because of the price that I have paid, you have a right to enter in, and bring your petitions before Me."* From that moment on, I knew my father would be alright.

Therefore, I dedicate this book to the Lord Jesus Christ, who made healing available because *"Who His own self bare our sins in His own body on the tree that we, being dead to sins, should live unto righteousness: by Whose stripes ye were healed."* I Peter 2:24. Only the Lord Jesus paid the price affording us all the blessings that relate to life and godliness. It is only through Him that we have eternal life.

I also dedicate this book to the many saints who have preached about the healing virtues made possible by the stripes that Jesus bore. They are worthy to be declared pioneers of faith. Many of those had to stand against false teachers who declared that miracles and supernatural healing had passed away with the Apostles.

Last, but not least, I dedicate this book to my sister-in-law, Darlene "Doll" Davis, who twice has typed the manuscript for "Do You Want To Get Well?" Although she was originally from West Virginia, she had to learn to read "Hill-Billy" Hieroglyphics in order to read my handwriting. August 2020

INTRODUCTION

I would like to introduce you to Darrell Davis, a Pastor, Evangelist, Teacher, Father, Grandfather, and Personal Friend. Over the last thirty-plus years I've known Darrell, he has maintained a constant dedication to growing in the knowledge of God and applying that knowledge to those he serves.

This book, *"DO YOU WANT TO GET WELL?"* addresses one of the foremost concerns of every person's life at some point. Every human is subject to many things in life - but sickness of self or loved ones brings endless worries, questions and panic. Sickness is one of Satan's most powerful weapons. However, knowing how to strategically combat the enemy is paramount at such a time. This book shows the spiritual techniques necessary for your success in any battle of illness leveled by Satan against the human body.

Pastor Darrell Davis has the credentials that are the most necessary for this type of book - experience. Darrell has selflessly and tirelessly served in various capacities of Ministry with the goal of always successfully bringing the real God to the entirety of the person: Body, Soul, and Spirit. Here in this book he achieves this.

This book will apply to you and those you love. You will be able to apply Scripture with better understanding and a clearer viewpoint of the application of Scripturally-Based Faith to your needs. Apply this to your life as one applies a Band-Aid to a cut or salve to a wound and see how you will grow in God and His Word.

Mike Smith, President & CEO
Living Faith Television
August 2020

FOREWORD

Do you want to get well? You can. Complete deliverance from sickness and continuing in good health is available to you. In this book we will look at God's Word to see just how this is possible.

Jesus asked an invalid man who was lying on a mat beside of the pool at Bethesda, ***"Do you really want to get well?"*** John 5:6. He was asking this of a man who had an infirmity (weakness or debilitating disease) for thirty-eight years. The disease was probably a type of paralysis, for the man said, ***"Sir, I have no man...to put me in the pool."*** He apparently needed help to move about. The nature of the disease is not the point, but that for the length of time that he was in that condition had all but made him give up hope of being the first to get into the pool, where he would be healed.

The Bible doesn't say, but we could draw our own

conclusions from experience, and from what is written, so that as Oral Roberts said, *"The man was lying down on the inside."* His faith was set on an event and not in God, the One who does the healing.

I suppose a question could be asked of the man in John 5, or of any of us: *"Once well, would he serve God, or not?"* Only God knows the heart and the obstacles which prevent or hinder The Healer from freely giving to us our health and healing. What about you? Do you really want to get well? Is there something standing in your way which blocks your deliverance from some sickness or disease? If so, perhaps there may be a spiritual or mental block such as the man had to whom Jesus has spoken.

The following is a list of some of the many barriers which can hinder us from receiving or accepting what is available to us:

*Do you believe in God? Yes or No?

*Do you believe He loves you? Yes or No?

*Do you believe God is a respecter of person? Yes or No?

*Do you believe God is Just? Yes or No?

*Do you believe God desires to bless those who are down and out, or sick? Yes or No?

These questions have to be resolved in our thinking concerning how we feel God thinks about us. After much prayer and study of the Holy Scriptures, my personal opinion is God desires to heal! He loves you as much as He does any of those mentioned in the Bible, but we must do what they did: EXERCISE FAITH IN A LOVING GOD.

There are many reasons why some people do not receive their healing. The greatest reason for not being healed is" the lack of knowledge", or false teaching.

The following is a list of teachings which have caused spiritual and mental blocks, or obstacles which have hindered multitudes from receiving what God desires to do for everyone. Please understand that any obstacles or hindrances, which prevent us from receiving God's blessings, through Jesus Christ, are first and foremost spiritual in nature. But for the sake of our understanding, these blocks have been divided into two groups: mental and spiritual blocks to healing.

"DO YOU WANT TO GET WELL?"
By DARRELL DAVIS

All scripture quotations are taken from the King James Version of the Holy Bible unless otherwise stated.

TABLE OF CONTENTS

MENTAL & SPIRITUAL BLOCKS TO HEALING

Mental Blocks to Healing:

1. If God loved me, He would heal me.

2. God heals only through doctors and medicine.

3. If it is His will. He will heal me.

4. God does not heal during this day and age.

5. My Church and Pastor/Preacher do not believe in divine healing.

6. I prayed once, but nothing happened, and now I do not believe.

7. I have committed the unpardonable sin.

8. I believe that it is God's will for me to be sick, and I am suffering for the Kingdom of God.

9. God is punishing me for some reason.

10. There are certain diseases and maladies which God chooses not to heal.

11. There are certain diseases and maladies which God cannot heal.

12. I hope to live good enough to deserve healing.

13. I have lived good all of my life, but I don't know why God doesn't heal me.

14. Being sick just must be my destiny.

15. God must be trying to teach me something and that is why this happened to me.

Spiritual Blocks to Healing:

1. Unbelief

2. Words of our mouth

3. Unforgiveness (My word used throughout this book)

4. Fear

Note:

 There are at least two things which must be established before you read any further.

First: Do you believe the Bible to be the Word of God? If you do, then proceed. If you do not believe the Bible to be the Word of God then the scriptures will serve to be a stumbling stone. Should you have any questions as to the authority of God's Word, ask God to clarify your understanding to the Bible and it's truths.

Second: You may need to ask yourself, *"Have I been born again or saved?"* If you are not, or you're not sure, then you are missing the greatest joy and power of a personal relationship with the Creator. But whether you are born again or not, if you will do what God says, using the Bible as your source of understanding, you too can be healed. The majority of those healed by Jesus were certainly not Christians. Say this with your mouth, as you believe in your heart,

"All scripture is given by the inspiration of God and is profitable for doctrine, for reproof, for correction, for instruction in righteousness: that the man of God may be perfect, thoroughly furnished unto all good works," II Timothy 3:16-17.

Do you believe all scripture is given by the inspiration of God? Have you tried just about everything, but you are not well? Then read this book with an open heart and I believe you will be in a better position to receive. In Section III, we learn how to get well after we have removed the mental and spiritual blocks which have kept us from receiving our healing.

SECTION I

Exposing Certain Teachings Which Have Kept People From Being Healed

CHAPTER ONE

If God Loved Me, He Would Heal Me

Do you believe God loves you? You may answer, *"I'm not really sure if God loves me."* Using the Bible as our only source of information, what do the scriptures teach us about God's love?

A. *"God is Love"*, I John 4:8. Whether you feel loved or not, it is still a written fact that God loves you.

B. *"For God so loved the world that He gave His only begotten Son..."* John 3:16.

C. *"But God commendeth (shows and proves) His Love toward us, in that, while we were yet sinners, Christ died for us"*. Romans 5:8.

Stop! Think about how God loves us, while we were yet sinners He sent Jesus Christ to die for our sins, because sin separated us from God. THAT IS LOVE. Sin blocked us from the blessings of God's love, but Jesus bridged the gap between God and humanity, and made all things possible to the believer.

D. *"Hereby perceive we the love of God, because he laid down His life for us*," I John 3:16.

E. *"Greater love hath no man than this that a man would lay down his life for his friends,"* John 15:13.

If He loves us enough to die for us and to wash away our sin, we must believe He loves us enough to make us well! It only stands to reason that anyone who loves us enough to lay down His life for us surely loves enough to help us, if He has the power to do so. Well, we know that God has the power, but we may not be sure of His willingness to heal us. Confess this with your mouth: ***"For God so loved the world."*** Let's make it more personal by inserting "me" for "world", and say it again. ***"For God so loved "me", that he gave His only begotten Son, that whosoever (that's me) believeth in Him should not perish but have everlasting life".*** John 3:16

Yes, according to the Word of God, Jesus loves you and me. When we accept God's Word at face value we can be assured of His love for us. This is faith. We receive God's love by faith, and know this: all blessings are received by the same faith, and healing is included.

Now if you are assured of His love according to the Bible, then allow Jesus to heal you.

CHAPTER TWO

God Heals Only Through Doctors and Medicine!

Does God use doctors and medicines as the only means of healing people today? NO! God can and will bless the use of doctors and medicines, but that is not His best. There will always be some pain and suffering, and failures where man and medicines are the only sources of healing. There are some very good medical practitioners but they do not have all of the answers.

We do know this earth was created and furnished with an abundance of health and healing in a wide variety of plants and herbs. From these many species of plants and herbs hundreds of medicines and vaccines have been developed, which has brought much relief and blessing to hurting humanity.

We find an example of a medicinal healing in the Bible, coupled with faith. In 2 Kings, chapter 20, it is recorded that King Hezekiah had a boil (ulcer and/or inflammation, perhaps turned gangrenous), and was dying. God sent Isaiah, the prophet to him with the message, ***"Set thy house in order, for thou shalt die and not live"***. As one would look closer, In II Chronicles 32:24-26, it is revealed why Hezekiah was sick unto death: his **Pride.**

Pride is sin, and sin is giving place to the devil, who is the author of sickness and disease. The thief comes to steal, kill, and destroy, and sin opens the door wide allowing the devil to enter and do his work. Pride in himself and his accomplishments had opened the door for the devil to afflict Hezekiah. Then Hezekiah turned his face to the wall and prayed unto the Lord. He humbled himself and repented of his pride, making a way for the blessings of God. For, you see, God resists the proud but gives grace to the humble. So, after the king's prayer of repentance; he cried out to the merciful God, who sent Isaiah with a message and a healing for his sickness.

In verse 5 of II Kings 20, God said, ***"I have heard thy prayer, I have seen thy tears: behold, I will heal thee."*** In verse 7, Isaiah told him, ***"take a lump of figs and they took and laid it on the boil and he recovered."***

The figs were used as a medicinal aid until his health returned. Through his faith and obedience God healed him. Doctors and medicines and fig poultices cannot heal but they can be used to treat the symptoms until healing is complete.

Hezekiah believed Isaiah's report, *"I will heal thee."* He believed! He received! He coupled his faith with the provision of healing made known to him. The figs were used to cover the sore, keeping it clean until he recovered. Well, certainly God will use medicines and doctors to minister to the needs of humanity, but He desires of us obedience and trust in Him as our Father, Provider, and Healer.

On the other hand look at II Chronicles 16:12, where King Asa trusted only in the doctors and he was diseased in his feet by an affliction, which ended in his death. The Bible says, *"Yet in his disease he sought not the Lord but to the physicians."* Shouldn't he have been healed?

King Asa was an ungodly man who had turned his back upon God; never putting his trust and confidence in the Lord God of Israel. During his sickness he repented of his sins but he did not look to God for healing. He was adamantly proud and stubborn and he depended upon man for his needs.

We must never try to live apart from God but be as willing as David was to *"Bless the Lord, O my soul, and forget not all his benefits: Who forgiveth all thine iniquities, who healeth all thy diseases."* Psalms 103: 2. Our reliance is in Jesus Christ. He alone is our source. There may not be anything wrong with the doctors, but be assured of this, God will be second to none!

Should you have neglected the Lord's provision for healing and have trusted only man and medicine, then repentance and confession is in order. Please pray this prayer with your mouth: *"Lord Jesus, please forgive*

me of pride, stubbornness, selfishness, and unbelief.
Jesus, I am sorry for not totally depending upon You.
I have been so hasty in seeking help of man, that I
have almost excluded You from the picture." "Lord
Jesus, I believe that You have forgiven me, according
to Your word, and I receive Your healing, In Jesus
Name."

If you can identify with any of the other teachings
listed in this section, which prevents you from
receiving your healing, then please continue with
Chapter 3, and be blessed; Or, if everything is cleared
up between you and God, turn to Chapter 20, read,
and believe for your healing.

CHAPTER THREE

If It Is His Will: He Will Heal Me

Are you one of those who believe, *"If it is God's will to heal me, He will heal me?"* Since the word healing is also translated the same as saved and prosperous, we may say it like this, *"If it is God's will to save me, He will."* Do you believe it is God's will to save people? Yes, or No? You and I know that it is God's will to save people. Why? Because Jesus came for that very purpose **"to seek and to save that which was lost"**. *Luke 19:10; II Peter 3:9 and I Timothy 2:4.*

These are a few of the scriptures that plainly teach us that God wants to save people. But, are all people going to be saved? No! Why not?

For whatever reason, there are many who will not come to Jesus to receive eternal life. Jesus said, **"...and him that cometh to me I will in no wise** *cast out."* *John 6:37.* Jesus also said in *John 5:40,* ***"And ye will not come to me, that ye might have life."*** God desires to save the world, but all men will not receive God's plan of salvation. God will save because He loves people.

According to the same Divine principle of love, God wants to deliver people from the bondage of sickness and disease, but all must come to Him and receive healing. Healing, as well as salvation, is available to one and all, but we have to be willing to come and partake of the goodness of the Lord. Let us look at one of the most profound examples of God's willingness to destroy the works of the devil.

In Mark, the very first chapter is the account of a leper who came to Jesus begging for help. Kneeling down he said to Jesus**, *"If thou wilt, thou canst make me clean.."*** And Jesus, moved with compassion (love), put forth his hand and touched him, and said unto him, ***"I WILL: be thou clean."*** Immediately the leprosy departed and the man was cleansed.

God is always willing to do good for us. In Acts 10:38, Peter speaks of Jesus, ***"Who went about doing good, and healing all that were oppressed of the devil; for God was with Him."*** God is willing to give, but, are we willing to receive what is provided? ***"Every good gift...is from above, and cometh down from the Father of lights..." James 1:16.*** We ***"must believe that He is, and that He is a rewarder of them that diligently seek Him."*** Hebrews 11:6.

Pay close attention to the beginning of the sixth chapter of Mark. It is in his hometown area that we see Jesus ministering to His very own neighbors and family. After all, wasn't He the hometown boy? Accepted? No! Rejected! Mark points out their unbelief blocked many miracles: ***"And He could there do no mighty work, save that He laid his hands upon a few sick folk, and healed them."*** The people of Nazareth reasoned in their minds, "that God could do miracles and perhaps be willing to heal and deliver the most noble or worthy, but surely He wouldn't do it that way, nor, would He use Jesus to do them." *"Everyone knew his mother was pregnant before marriage."*

Unbelief smothered out any hope of seeing the miraculous performed in the little village of Nazareth. I wonder if we are any different today? We seem to know that God "can do anything", and yet, we doubt his methods and choices. God is willing to do great wonders and miracles. Jesus was willing to deliver them. Are we willing and eager to receive from His bountiful hand? Do we say we believe in our prayer-closets while doubt festers in our hearts and flows from the end of the tongue like rivers? It is God's good pleasure to give us the Kingdom, and in the Kingdom is health and healing.

Do you believe that God will heal you? Should you have doubted His willingness to heal you, and you have a desire to repent? Please repeat these words from the heart: *"Lord Jesus, please forgive me because I did not believe that You were willing to heal me. I am sorry for doubting Your compassion and love. I thank You for your forgiveness, and I receive it right now, In Jesus Name."*

This would be an excellent time for you to lift your hands and begin to praise the Lord. Now, if you have cleared up any misunderstanding concerning God's will to heal you, then turn to chapter 20, and continue with your healing. But, should there be a nagging question in your mind about anything discussed to this point, or if you think that God doesn't heal today, go to the next chapter for some help. Do not skip one single page.

CHAPTER FOUR

God Does Not Heal Today

God used to heal people, but now there isn't a need to have healing. Therefore healing has been taken out of God's promises. We have the Bible and miracles aren't needed to establish God's plan of redemption today. Have you heard these statements?
Let me ask you a few simple questions.

When did God stop healing people who were sick?

When did He stop casting out devils?

When did He stop saving people?

When did God stop performing miracles?

Did healing really stop with the Apostles, or the early church?

God never concluded at any time in the Bible, that after the death of the Apostles, all miracles would cease. Neither the apostles nor disciples healed one person. The name of Jesus was used by those who believed, and *"the Lord worked with them, confirming the Word of God with signs and wonders."* Mark 16:20.

There were some very powerful promises made by Jesus just before His ascension, as stated by Mark, chapter sixteen, and Mark quoted Jesus, who *"These signs shall follow them that believe; in my name shall they cast out devils; they shall speak with new tongues; they shall take up serpents; and if they drink any deadly thing, it shall not hurt them; they shall lay hands on the sick, and they shall recover."*

Signs would follow who? The believers! Also, signs will follow any who would use the name of Jesus, doubting nothing. If believers cannot do these things, then believers cannot be saved. Because in the same chapter, Jesus also said, *"Go into all the world, and preach the Gospel to every creature. All who believe and will be baptized will be saved, and these signs shall follow them."* (Paraphrase). Jesus worked with the apostles and disciples for three and one-half years. He taught them, showing them by example: how to pray, heal the sick, cast out devils, and *"as my Father has sent me even so send I You."* These are the words of Jesus. John 20:21.

In Matthew 28:19-20, Jesus told the disciples to *"go into all the world, and teach all nations to observe whatsoever he had commanded*

them." In John 14:12-14, He told his disciples that they would do **"greater works"** than what He had done. They would use his name and the Father would do whatever "they asked." In Acts of the Apostles, not only did the Apostles carry out Jesus' commands, but many disciples were used by God to fulfill the great commission.

Part of the great commission is to preach the Gospel, which **"is the power of God unto salvation."** Jesus told them to preach the Gospel, and they were to teach others to observe all that He had commanded them, according to Matthew 28:19-20. We must do the same work and preach the same Gospel as the early church.

Many skeptics think that God stopped loving people. God has not stopped loving people. Or, that God has changed. Really? God still loves, saves, heals, baptizes in the Holy Spirit, delivers, cast out devils and blesses, where faith is acted upon. In Hebrews 13:8, it plainly declares, **"Jesus Christ the same yesterday, and today, and forever."** Go back and search through the Old Testament. Did God do miracles? Did He heal people? Did He raise the dead? Yes! We know He did! God worked miracles in the Old Testament. He did not stop in the New Testament, and to be sure, He will not stop until the last enemy has been put under the feet of Jesus (death), and God's will totally fulfilled.

Should you be one of those who believed God does not heal today, you need to ask God to forgive you. Say this, with an open heart, *"Lord Jesus, please forgive me for not believing in Your love toward me. I doubted Your word. Would You forgive me? You have never changed Lord Jesus, but man has changed. Please forgive us for changing Your word. I receive, now, Your forgiveness, and I receive Your healing, in Jesus name."*

If you believe that all obstacles, which have kept you from receiving your healing, have been removed, then proceed to Chapter 20, and be healed in Jesus name. However, if you have been guilty of any of the other teachings listed in the introduction, then please continue to read. You do not have anything to lose, but you have healing to gain.

CHAPTER FIVE

My Church Does Not Believe In Healing

I have tried to "get" my healing, but my pastor, church; family, friends and denomination do not believe it. What do I do? Just because most did not believe in Jesus' message, did that stop Him from fulfilling the Father's will and continuing His mission to the cross? No! Even if the majority of the people did not believe in Jesus, period, did that make Jesus wrong? No!

Suppose some do not believe for whatever reason, does that stop healing from being made available? No! Jesus told the disciples that He would rise from the dead after three days. How many believed Him? NONE! Jesus told the disciples to go and tarry until they be **"endued with the power"** of the Holy Spirit. How many believed his words? About one hundred and twenty; where were all those thousands who followed Him?

Listen beloved, you read God's Word and believe for yourself and be healed. If John the "Cold Christian" of today doesn't believe, so what? You believe and receive whatever you ask for.

What do airline pilots talk about? Flying, would you not think so? What do bankers converse about? Money? What do teachers speak about? Teaching the students? Whatever an individual's profession might be, if they are successful, they will talk about their profession. I wonder what unbelievers talk about? Do you think they sit around and talk about faith? NO! They talk unbelief. Now if you keep hanging around where unbelief is spoken and acted upon, what do you think will happen to you? You will become a professional nonbeliever.

Did you ever stop and think what it would be like if you played on a professional football team? Then suppose that all you ever said to the other players was, *"I don't believe we can win." "We cannot possibly win." "Why bother to play ball, we will probably get beaten so bad anyway, we will look foolish." "We are not that good."* On and on and on, you kept talking defeatism. How long do you think the coach would allow you to play ball? Never, is right.

Your attitude would be all wrong; your attitude would poison those around you. Has your attitude about healing been poisoned? If so, do this: Pray these words. *"Lord Jesus, please forgive me for allowing those around me to shape my attitude toward You and healing. I was convinced that You did not heal, today, and I did not search the Bible for myself. I receive Your forgiveness for my error, and I will not let those around me poison my faith in You any longer, In Jesus Name."* Hallelujah!

If you have cleared all differences with your Heavenly Father, proceed to chapter 20, for your total healing. But, if you are still plagued with some of the teachings which are given in Section I, please do not despair. Would you read on a little further? Jesus has something special just for you.

CHAPTER SIX

Prayed Once, but Nothing Happened

I prayed about my healing once, but nothing seemed to happen, so I quit praying. I simply do not believe anymore. Well, you began on the right track, but welcome to the world of human beings. Every one of us have faced similar problems, and received the same results. Nothing! Or, so it seemed to us at the time.

It had been said that Winston Churchill, when asked to address a graduating class of Oxford University, said, ***"Never, give up! Never, give up! Never, give up!"*** It was reported that was all he said. That was enough. Anyone listening would have received the message. (Author's note: The speech that Churchill gave was at a high school where he attended years before, and parts were repeated at other events).

Jesus spoke of a parable, in Luke Chapter Eighteen,

about how men ought to always pray, and not to faint. Faint means to lose heart, or give up; we are to pray without ceasing. If you believe, then do not stop believing. Keep on believing! Jesus said in Mark 9:23, ***"If thou canst believe, all things are possible to him that believeth."*** Just because you did not see any real change in your condition that did not mean your healing had not begun. This is why we are going through these steps and procedures.

God wants you to receive what you are believing Him for. Do you know that when Jesus said, ***"They shall lay hands upon the sick, and they shall recover,"*** that word ***"recover"*** means to get well, or be well? They shall be well; a process of recovery. Healing may be instantaneous. Other times, it may be over a period of time before we are fully restored.

The main thing is to continue to seek God, believing that He wants you to be well. Psalms 34:10, the last of the verse states, ***"...but they that seek the Lord shall not want any good thing."*** Seek, here, implies to tread around, or to tread often to a place, frequent, etc. Hence, to tread, or to frequent the Lord often because you desire to be with Him: Psalms 16:11, declares, ***"thou wilt show me the path of Life: in thy presence is fullness of joy; at thy right hand there are pleasures for evermore."***

Come often before the Lord, and seek to know Him. He will, in return, completely satisfy you with His very presence, which will bring joy, healing, truth, love, holiness, and blessings untold. But, more than seeking Him to obtain His blessings, rather seek Him for His fellowship and companionship. Recall that Matthew 6:33, teaches ***"But seek ye first the Kingdom of***

God, and His righteousness; and all these things shall be added unto you".

Should you have been one of those people who had begun believing for healing but had given up hope, if so, then please do something about it. Say these words with your mouth:

"Dear Lord Jesus, please forgive me for my unbelief. Strengthen me. Holy Spirit, lead me right now that I may know how to pray correctly. I now receive your forgiveness and cleansing of the sin of unbelief. I receive my healing, In Jesus Name."

If you are clear of all doubt and unbelief about your healing, then go to Chapter 20, and continue to pray. If you are still having a problem with any of the teachings in this section, then please continue on to the next chapter. Do not give up!

CHAPTER SEVEN

I Have Committed the Unpardonable Sin

I have committed the unpardonable sin, and therefore God will not forgive me and heal me. Who said that you had committed the unpardonable sin? Do you know what the unpardonable sin is?

What is commonly referred to as the unpardonable sin is mentioned in Matthew 12:22-23. Jesus was speaking out because a certain religious faction had accused Him of casting out devils by the power of Beelzebub, the prince of devils. In other words, the power of an unclean spirit was thought to be working through Jesus. He told them *"and whosoever speaks a word against the Son of man, it shall be forgiven him: but whosoever speaks against the Holy Ghost, it shall not be forgiven him, neither in this world, neither in the world to come."*

If you reject the Holy Spirit, and declare Him to be unclean, or have demoralized His character in any way, then that is blaspheming the Holy Spirit. Telling the Holy Spirit never to convict you, or to demand Him to leave you and never come back to you, would be a case in point of rejection. The Holy Spirit would probably never come back to you. But, that would be up to God.

Now, of course God knows whether you meant what you said. Have you ever said or committed such acts against the Holy Spirit that could be identified with real rejection and blasphemy? I would venture a guess and say that "you probably have never even entertained the thought of ever abusing the Holy Spirit." So go on from here and be blessed of God by reading His word and communing daily with Him in prayer.

CHAPTER EIGHT

God's Will Is To Be Sick

*"It must be His will for me to be sick and suffering,"
you say.* Do you really believe that? Do you think that
God is actually going to make you sick just so you can
suffer for Him? What good would it do if Jesus and
the rest of the world allowed you to be sick? When you
are sick, you are not going to be a blessing to anyone,
and certainly not to your family. Much of the money
that you need to buy food, clothing, pay for utilities,
etc., is spent on your doctors and medicine in an
attempt to get well. If this is God's will for you to be
sick, wouldn't you be doing wrong by going to the
doctor in your attempt to get well? You would be
trying to get well against God's will. By natural
instinct all of us try to do everything possible to get
well, and ask God to be our helper.

Do you think God gets any satisfaction out of your

being sick? What kind of a mad creature would get his kicks out of babies being born deformed, or children suffering from diseases and malnutrition? What good would it do anyone to lie on a bed of sickness, dying of some horrible illness, body wracked with pain, bleeding from the eyes, nose, ears and mouth? Who is that going to help? **No one**!

Jesus taught the disciples how to pray. And in Matthew 6:10, in His prayer, He says, ***"Thy will be done in earth, as it is in heaven."*** Do you think it is God's will for there to be sickness in heaven? NO, of course not; well, why would you think it would be His will for there to be sickness in the earth? It is not His will.

We realize that a curse was brought to bear upon a fallen world because of sin. Where sin is, a law of cursing is in operation. But Romans 8:2, says, ***"For the law of the Spirit of life in Christ Jesus has made me free from the law of sin and death."*** Paul wrote in a letter to the Galatians, ***"Christ has redeemed us from the curse of the law being made a curse for us: for it is written, cursed is every one that hangeth on a tree (cross): that the blessing of Abraham might come on the Gentiles through Jesus Christ: that we might receive the promise of the Spirit through faith."*** Notice, he said, ***"Christ has redeemed us from the curse...that the blessing of Abraham might come..."***

He said a blessing and not a curse. Is sickness, disease, suffering, etc. a blessing or a curse? It is a curse! It is not God's will for people to suffer sickness, diseases, wars, famines, plagues, and such things, but they are all around us. So long as we have a world in rebellion against God, such will continue to happen throughout the world. The only way of escape is coming to God and giving Jesus our whole heart. God will heal, save, deliver, rescue and redeem man only when man cries out to Him in faith.

Jesus has already once and for all settled the problems and failures associated with sin. We have to receive His forgiveness of sin, and the provisions paid for by Jesus Christ's death, burial, and resurrection.. Our healing and deliverance has already been taken care of, but we have to receive His gifts by faith. Our healing and deliverance has already been taken care of, but we have to believe Him and receive what is available. It is not whether God wills it or not, for we know His will by reading His word.

In Isaiah 1:19, God says, ***"If we be willing and obedient ye shall eat the good of the land."*** Are we willing? God has always been willing to do good. Man is the one who is unwilling. Willingness is our responsibility. Are you willing to believe God? Are you willing to ask God to forgive you for thinking that He would be pleased to make people sick? If so, then let us confess our sins of ignorance. *"Precious Lord Jesus, I have been so ignorant of Your word. Would You please forgive me for accusing You of "willing" people to be sick and afflicted? You came to heal people and set them free, and not bring people further suffering and sorrow. Please cleanse me of the religious misunderstanding, and I will never again think it is Your will for people to suffer untold misery, In Jesus Name."*

Right now, receive His forgiveness by faith. Thank

Him for His mercy and forgiveness. He is the wonderful and loving Heavenly Father. If you have gotten that teaching all straight, and you believe all is well, then turn to Chapter 20, and get free from whatever it is that is tormenting you. If you know in your heart, however, that some bad teaching is still lingering in your thinking, then let us proceed to the next problem area.

CHAPTER NINE

God Is Punishing Me

"God is punishing me for some reason, this is why I must be sick, but if I have done anything, I don't know what it could be." Is that the way you feel? Why would God want to punish you with some devastating disease or crippling infirmity?

Is that how you would punish one of your children? Would you afflict them for all of their lives with a crippling disease or affliction? No, and a thousand times no! You would never do that. Neither does God try to destroy people with terrible diseases. He does not punish or even chastise people with maladies and so forth, in order to teach them.

In Hebrews 12: 5-6, which states, ***"..and ye have forgotten the exhortation which speaketh unto you as unto children, my son, despise*** *not thou the chastening of the Lord, nor faint when thou are rebuked of Him: for whom the Lord loveth He chasteneth, and scourgeth every son whom he receiveth."* Notice the *word chasteneth;* which means to train children, and to educate them, and to instruct them until they come into full possession of salvation, or whatever they are being trained for.

Now, there is one thing certain, God may permit a few things to happen to us, especially if we are in disobedience. He may permit trials and temptations and troubles, but He doesn't teach us by smiting us with the devil's dirty tricks.

Let me explain what I mean. In John 10:10, the thief is the one who comes to steal, and to kill and to destroy. But on the other hand, Jesus said, *"I have come that you might have life."* Jesus didn't come to destroy us, but to give us life. If you read the first two chapters of Job, the picture of who destroys and kills will become clearer to you. *"The devil goes about seeking whom he may devour".* I Peter 5:8-9. Do you know what you can do to the devil? Resist him!

That's right, just resist him and he will flee from you, which is what James 4:7, and I Peter 5:8-9 tells us. We are to resist the devil, not pet him. In Matthew 4, the tempter came to Jesus, but Jesus resisted him with the written Word of God. Listen up! If the devil comes near and you let him push you around, jump on your kids, make you sick, steal finances, steal your family, bring temptations, then God will also let him do those things. GOD GAVE US AUTHORITY OVER THE DEVIL AS WE USE JESUS' NAME!

If you permit the devil to push you around, so will God. Remember what happened in the garden, east of Eden? In Genesis 3: The devil came around, and Adam and Eve listened to the jerk. If you do what the devil says, he will kill you. If you leave him free course, he will do you great harm.

"Well, why didn't God do something about it?", you ask. He did. He gave Adam the authority to keep the garden and the right to tell the devil to get out. Adam failed to exercise his authority. Furthermore, God isn't going to override your free will. Satan will push you, and shove you, and drive you until there is nothing left. God will not, and never has operated like that.

God always guides us by his Spirit, Who is known as the **"Spirit of Truth!"** In John 16:13, Jesus said, **"Howbeit when he, the Spirit of Truth, is come, he will guide you into all truth...**" God leads us into truth and not into destruction.

Should you ever walk in disobedience and rebellion, you will be in deep trouble. Disobedience and rebellion is in the devil's territory, and he plays dirty. If you walk away from God and His protection and get over on the devils territory of sin, you are on your own. The Holy Spirit is exactly that; **"Holy"** and He doesn't hang around the devil's territory. If you, or anyone, gives place to the devil, the Holy Spirit will not be around. For the Holy Spirit will not commit sin. The Holy Spirit leads out of sin, not into it. Sin is the devil's territory.

No, God hasn't punished you with some kind of sickness, such as cancer, just so you may suffer. I believe if you ask God to heal you, He would. For in

Exodus 15:26, the last part of the verse it says, ***"...for I am the Lord that healeth thee."*** Right now we have grace, but judgment and punishment will come later to those who reject the Lord Jesus as Savior.

Now, if you were one of those who had been thinking all along that God was chastising you with sickness for whatever reason, then you need to pray this, *"Dear Lord Jesus, I have been wrong for so long. I did not know that You were not chastening me with this foul disease and infirmity. Would You forgive me? I receive Your forgiveness, right now Lord, in Jesus name. Thank You, Jesus, for forgiving and cleansing me by Your Word and Spirit."*

Well, have you removed all the religious and mental blockages from between you and the Father? If so, continue to Chapter 20, and do not forget to pray. If there are other unresolved issues, proceed to the next chapter please, and be healed in Jesus Name.

CHAPTER TEN

God Doesn't Heal Certain Diseases

Maybe there are certain diseases which God had chosen not to heal, and what if I have one of those diseases? Why would God choose to heal only a few select diseases and not all of them? Would you read Acts 10:38, right now? What does it say? *"...Jesus...who went about doing good and healing all that were oppressed of the devil..."* Sicknesses, diseases, and such are oppressions of the devil. The devil comes to steal, kill, and destroy.

Now, 1 John 3:8b, *"For this purpose the son of God was manifested, that he might destroy the works of the devil."* If Jesus was going to heal all and destroy the works of the devil, then He has to heal all who are sick, cleanse all the sinners, etc., who come to Him.

And Praise God, Jesus has come to give us life through His shed blood, and through His death, burial, and resurrection. Yes, God will heal all diseases and infirmities, and any problem that you may have. Go to the Father on the strength of His love for you and receive your healing, forgiveness, and whatever you need.

Ask Jesus, right now to forgive you for any and all sin if you have doubted Him. *"Lord Jesus, forgive me for doubting whether or not You would heal me. Your word says that **"all things are possible to him that believeth"**, and I believe You have forgiven me. So, I receive Your forgiveness and healing, in Jesus name."* Thank Him for His cleansing and healing. Turn to chapter 20, and continue in healing. After going over the list of false ideas and/or teachings of man that are shown in Section 1, and if there seems to be other problem areas in your thinking, then please continue to read. Do not despair; hang in there, for healing is yours in Jesus Name.

CHAPTER ELEVEN

God Cannot Heal Certain Diseases

Are there diseases which are incurable, even for God? No! Jesus said in Matthew 28:18, ***"All power is given unto me in heaven and in the earth."*** He has all power, and it is available to the believer. Moreover, do not forget what has been said in Acts 10:38, He "...***went about doing good and healing all who were oppressed of the devil, for God was with Him."***

If God did not want everyone healed, then He sent the wrong person when He sent Jesus: Because Jesus healed them all!

If you would turn to Luke 13 and read verses 11 through 17, you will see the contrast between the work of God and the devil's work. The devil had bound that poor (lack of physical health) woman with a spirit of infirmity for over eighteen years. For eighteen long years she had suffered at the hands of the enemy of man. Jesus saw her, He laid His hands on her and she was immediately made straight. Isn't that wonderful? He will also make you well by His love and power. What the devil messes up, Jesus straightens up.

Think about this. Whatever the enemy can mess up, you know that God can and will fix up. The God that we serve spoke and brought everything into being according to Psalms 33:6, and Hebrews 11:2. Hebrews 1:3 says, **"and upholding all things by the Word of His power."** After all, do you know that, **"He sent His Word and healed them,"**? Psalms 107:20. His word was sent to heal spirit, soul, and body of man, as well as anything else that needed to be restored.

God is all powerful and cannot fail.

Ask God to forgive you, right now, for making Him such a small God. *"Lord Jesus, please forgive me for even doubting Your greatness. You are omnipotent (all powerful), and since You are all powerful, You will forgive and heal me. I receive that forgiveness in Jesus name."*

Turn to chapter 20, when you are sure all doubt is gone as to God's ability to heal all manner of sicknesses, and diseases. If you do not have peace in your heart concerning your healing, then please read further. By God's grace, He will bring you to the place where you can totally depend upon His love and power.

CHAPTER TWELVE

I Hope To Live Good Enough

Have you ever felt like that, or thought it? Or, perhaps you've said, *"I'm so unworthy for Jesus to heal me, or bless me."* Well, you are absolutely right. Not one of us is "worth his salt", the old timers used to say. We could never deserve heaven, or Jesus dying for us, or any of God's blessings, no matter how good we try to live.

Besides, it isn't how good we live, but it is what Jesus has done for us. He came into this world to pay the price of our sins and shortcomings with God. We were all hell deserving sinners until Jesus Christ shed His precious blood to wash away our sins. Salvation, healing, baptism of the Holy Spirit, and all other blessings are gifts from God. We don't earn them, but we receive them.

Read James 1:17, in your Bible. Notice that it says; ***"Every good gift and every perfect gift is from above, and cometh down from the father of lights..."*** We do not earn gifts. Healing is a gift.

Likewise, in 1 Corinthians 12:9, one of the gifts of the Holy Spirit (special supernatural endowments) is the ***"gifts of healing."*** The ability to minister healing to others is a gift as well, and the healing itself is a gift. In Acts 2:38, the Holy Spirit is a gift, and to be sure, all that is given by Him is a gift.

In this life, we will probably never live good enough to deserve all that God wants to give us. But, we can believe by faith in His promises and receive the benefits of them. Even though ***"we have all sinned and come short of His glory",*** Jesus paid our penalty of sin, and has made us worthy to receive from God. In Hebrews 2:11, he went so far as to say, ***"for which cause he is not ashamed to call them brethren."*** And in Romans 8:14-17, we are called ***"children of God, heirs; heirs of God, and joint heirs with Christ."***

Have you given your life over to God? If you have, then you are an heir of His. If you are an heir of God, then you are in line to receive all that God has for you. Plead the blood of Jesus Christ over your life, right now. And pray this out loud with your mouth. *"Lord Jesus, I thank You for taking my place on the cross. I deserve death and hell for I too have sinned. But You took my place, by laying down Your life for me, shedding Your blood to cleanse me of my sins, and wrote my name in the Book of Life. Because You paid for my debt, I am now worthy to be called a child of God. Thank You for it. I now receive Your gift of healing, in Jesus name."*

Do you feel better? It is good to know that we are saved because of Jesus' free gift, and we are also healed by His free gift. If you have prayed and all of those nagging thoughts of un-worthiness are gone, then proceed to Chapter 20, and be healed. If you know that some troubled area is still in your thinking, then please continue: for God wants you well more than you do.

CHAPTER THIRTEEN

I Have Lived Good Enough

I have lived good all of my life, but I do not know why God does not heal me. This sad fact is, many people feel the same way, and they also are not healed. As stated earlier, healing is a gift and not something to be earned by good works.

Another fact is that you are in an area of unbelief. *"You do not know why God does not heal you"*, is one of the great statements of unbelief. Turn your Bible to Mark 5:25-34, and read the account of the woman who had the issue of blood. For twelve years she has suffered many things, or suffered many kinds of treatments, at the hands of doctors, but she became worse.

Then she heard that Jesus was in town, and in verse 28, she said, ***"If I may touch but his clothes, I***

shall be whole." The next verse reveals that the flow of blood was immediately dried up.

Let me ask you a question, if I may? Was her sickness healed because she touched Jesus' clothes, or because of her faith? Of course it was her faith. Many people touched Jesus, but were not healed because they did not have that kind of faith, nor put faith into action.

Notice verse 34, where Jesus stated the reason that she was healed. He said unto her, ***"daughter, thy faith hath made thee whole; go in peace and be whole of thy plague."*** Her faith rested in Jesus' ability to make her whole. She believed and said; ***"If I may touch but his clothes, I shall be whole."*** Listen, you will probably never touch Jesus physically in this life, but you can: TOUCH HIM WITH YOUR FAITH.

Almost every healing situation, in the days of Jesus' ministry, involved the faith of the person who needed healing. Your healing will also depend upon your attitude about healing, and your faith will have to be involved. Jesus is not going to heal you just because you live good. Now don't misunderstand what I am saying. Yes, God could heal you anyway, for He is God. But more than likely you will not receive your healing because you live "good enough". I think you need to examine yourself to see if you are living in an area of spiritual pride. I mean, after all, "you have lived good enough."

Have you ever heard people make the statement, *"If ole so-and-so makes it to heaven, I don't have anything to worry about!"*? This is called pride. Our salvation, or healing, or any blessing from God will not be obtained by our attitude of "good living." We must never compare ourselves, or our religious experiences, with what Jesus has accomplished for us. Jesus is the one who has paid all of the debts and obtained all of the benefits for us. And these benefits are free.

Psalms 84:11, says, *"..No good thing will He* (God) *withhold from them that walk uprightly."*

The writer is not saying that a person will receive anything from God on the basis of his walking upright, but rather his upright position is one of walking with God and asking to receive through faith. *"The just shall live by faith",* and not "live" because he is inherently good.

Psalms 34:10 says, *"...but they that seek the Lord shall not want any good thing."* Psalms 37:4, teaches us to *"delight thyself in the Lord; also and he shall give you the desires of your heart.".* But notice the preceding verse 3, it says to, *"trust* (have faith*) in the Lord, and do good, so shalt thou dwell in the land, and verily thou shalt be fed."*

So, living good isn't enough to be healed, but to *trust, seek*, and/or have *faith* in the Lord.

The verses of Psalms 34:19 and 37:4, say to *"seek"* and to *"delight"* in the Lord and then He (Lord) will minister to us good things, but we *cannot please God* without faith.

Of course, living good is desirable with God, for He desires for all of the world to live good. But, God wants us to live a life full of faith and trust in him. He wants to be our source of supply for all of our wants and needs. Forget about receiving because you live good, and begin to concentrate on receiving from God by faith. A humble attitude toward God, coupled with faith in what Jesus has acquired for us, and asking God on that basis will get results for you.

Results! That is what we want. Amen? Ask God to forgive you for any spiritual pride which you may have. Pray out loud this prayer: *"Dear Lord Jesus, please forgive me for any spiritual pride, which I may knowingly or unknowingly possessed. I'm sorry for this sin. Would You wash me and make me whole? I thank You right now for forgiveness. I receive it in Jesus' name. I confess that Jesus is the only one who has ever 'lived right', and I therefore receive His righteousness; In Jesus name."*

If you feel that your attitude has been a hindrance to you, and that God has forgiven you, please turn to Chapter 20, and be well in Jesus name. If you still aren't free, please continue to the next chapter, and let Jesus fix you up right. OK?

CHAPTER FOURTEEN

Sickness Is My Destiny

This is my destiny. I must bear this sickness and malady for the remainder of my days. Wherein the Bible did you read that? No, you did not read that in your Bible.

Now, there have been many times that people have gotten over into certain areas of rebellion and disobedience, and because of it they had to suffer. However, most of the time if they had only repented and obeyed God, and asked for healing, they would have received it. God is a God of restoration, and not a God of hatred and unforgiving. God is interested in restoring people and not destroying them.

There are many scriptures in the Bible contrasting the righteous man and the wicked man. There is a vast difference between the two, and a vast difference in the way they will be treated in this life and the life to come. One Psalm that clearly makes a distinction between the righteous and the wicked is Psalms 37:38, *"The transgressors* (sinners) *shall be destroyed together: the end of the wicked shall be cut off. "*

On the other hand, the writer says in verse 39, *"But the salvation* (deliverance, safety, welfare, help, aid, victory) *of the righteous is of the Lord; he is their strength in the time of trouble".*

God is a helper to the righteous man any time he is in trouble. God helps him now, and not just when he gets ready to die. David said in Psalms 46:1, *"God is our refuge and strength, a very present help in trouble." "This poor man cried, and the Lord heard him, and saved* (delivered) *him out of all his troubles,"* Psalms 34:6. If God had destined David to be afflicted all of his life, there would not have been any reason for David to have prayed. I mean, Why pray if God had said, *"Your destiny cannot be changed; you must remain the same?"*

In verse 19, same chapter, he went on to say, *"Many are the afflictions of the righteous; but the Lord delivereth* (saves*) him out of them all."* Thank God for healing and deliverance.

Consider the same kind of thinking, but this time, apply that to salvation. *"Well, I suppose that I am destined to go to hell. Hell must be my destiny."* You say, *"That's ridiculous. No one has been made just to go to hell."*

No matter how radical it may sound to you, there are

people who are taught it and believe it.

They go to the grave believing that it is not God's will to save them. They need only read 1 Timothy 2:4, and 2 Peter 3:9, and know that God's will is for every man to be saved.

It is a lie of the devil that gives people the idea of an unchangeable destiny. Ideas like that are found in occults and astrology; which never originated with God. If we could never have a choice in the matter of serving God or not, then faith would be useless and void.

Faith denotes trust, and it speaks of a relationship based upon love. We determine our destinies by our faith in the Lord Jesus Christ. Jesus gave us His Word about eternal life and the future. If we receive that Word into our hearts by faith, then we can be born again and our future dwelling place changes. Heaven and Hell are determined by our acceptance or rejection of Jesus' words.

Well, trust Him. We are saved if we have heard and believed the preached word, this is the real story of love. Faith is believing His words of love. God loves us, and we can choose to believe it or not. If anyone could have justified the "destiny" theory as applying to theirs, it would have been those people who were born with a handicap.

For instance, John 9, the blind man, who was born without sight. He, as well as others, thought some terrible sin had been committed, and he was destined to remain in darkness forever. But, glory to God, Jesus healed him.

Also look in Mark 10:46-52, is the record of blind Bartimaeus, and how he sat beside of the road begging. Destiny wasn't on the blind man's mind, but getting healed was. He cried out and Jesus said to him, ***"Go thy way, they faith hath made thee whole."*** Faith in Jesus' words changed what would have been Bartimaeus' destiny.

Faith overrides what the devil has destined for us! Rise up and be healed, in Jesus name. Forget about being destined to bear some lie of the devil, and be whole in Our Lord's wonderful name!

In Deuteronomy 30:19-20, God said, ***"I call heaven and earth to record this day against you, that I have set before you life and death, blessing and cursing: Therefore choose life, that both thou and they seed may live: that thou mayest obey his voice, and that thou might cleave unto him: for He is thy life, and the length of thy days..."*** Praise God beloved, choose life, and not some poor picture of death and despair. You have a choice; use it for your sake. Ask God to forgive you if you have been plagued with this kind of teaching.

Pray out loud this short prayer. *"Dear Lord Jesus, I have listened to the devil and his lies long enough. Please forgive me for doubting Your willingness to heal me. I renounce this false destiny idea right now. This sickness and disease is not my lord, but Jesus you are my Lord, and my destiny. Jesus, You have given me a right to choose, and I now take that right. I choose to serve You, and I choose health. I receive Your forgiveness by faith, in Jesus name."*

It always feels better after prayer, and if you know that God wants you to be well, then turn to Chapter 20, and receive your healing from Jesus. For additional reasons why people are not healed, continue reading in the following chapters.

CHAPTER FIFTEEN

God Must Be Trying To Teach Me Something

God must be trying to teach me something, and that is why this happened to me. Have you been harangued by such thoughts as these? Would you take your child's hand and stick it into a hot stove just to teach it 'that the stove is hot'? No, how ridiculous it would be to burn and scar the child's hand for life just to show it that a stove is hot. Damaging the child physically and emotionally to teach it a lesson, is that your way?

God does not lead us by making us sick, or killing our kids, or stealing our money, or giving us cancer, taking our health, and burning down our house, etc. No, what kind of God would lead his people by destroying them?

Jesus said, in John 16:13, *"Howbeit when he, the Spirit of truth is come, he will guide you into all truth."* Jesus leads us by his Holy Spirit and not by destruction. For the prophet Hosea wrote, *"My people are destroyed for lack of knowledge..."* Hosea 4:6. We invite trouble when we forsake God and His commandments. If we forsake God we become open game for the devil to destroy us. Note 1 Peter 5:8, *"Be sober, be vigilant, for adversary the devil, as a roaring lion walketh about seeking whom he may destroy."* and in John 10:10, Jesus said, *"The thief cometh not but for to steal, and to kill, and to destroy."* Our enemy is the devil. He hates God and he hates man.

Anyone reading the story of Job quickly sees that Satan was the one who tempted Job to curse God to His face. Open your Bible and read Job 1:11, and realize who was the real enemy. The devil stirred up the Sabeans, who stole Job's oxen and asses. In verse 16, Job's servants claimed that the fire of God fell from heaven and burned up Job's sheep and servants. Was it the fire of God or the fire of the devil that fell upon Job's property?

Chaldean raiders under Satan's influence stole Job's camels and killed his servants. A great wind from the wilderness smote the house where Job's children were having a drinking party, and they were all killed. In one day's time Job lost all of his possessions, children and most of his servants. Later, he was even afflicted with boils over his entire body. What more could have been worse for Job?

But, did God do those things? No, the devil came to destroy Job. Job loved and served God, but Satan did not like it. In Job 42:10, it says that the Lord turned Job's captivity, and gave him twice as much as he had before. Praise God! For God is the one who restores good things to mankind.

If Job learned a lesson out of all his trails, it would have been these two things:

1.) The devil is responsible for destroying people's lives,

And

2.) God will make everything turn out all right, if one will put their trust in Him.

To my point, it wasn't necessary for the Lord to afflict Job to teach him to be a kind and generous person. Job fed the poor and helped those around him long before his trial.

Today, God uses apostles, prophets, evangelists, pastors, and teachers to help us mature into the perfection, or completion, or maturity of spiritual adulthood. Ephesians 4:11-13. Sickness isn't to be our teacher. The Holy Spirit is the One Who leads us into all truth. Also turn to 2 Timothy 3:16-17, where it plainly says that God used the scriptures to correct us and to instruct us. The scriptures and ministers, quickened by the Holy Spirit, is God's method for teaching us to know the truth about Christian conduct in this life.

However, be sure of this one thing, God will take advantage of our troubles to begin to speak to our hearts. He will gently speak to us and say, ***"I have*** *come that you might have life and that you may have it more abundantly."* Jesus always moves toward us with compassion, and seeks to heal our bruises, lift us from Satan's pits, and establish our steps.

Jesus taught in Matthew 7:24-27, *"Whosoever builds his life upon My word when the storms of life come, he will not fail."* (Paraphrase) *"But everyone who hears and refuses My Word, just as surely as the storms that will come, his life will fall apart."* (Paraphrase)

Do you recall in Mark 6:1-6, when Jesus returned to his boyhood town, how the majority of the people rejected him? *"He could not work mighty miracles there because of their unbelief. Only a few had faith to believe in Him."* (Paraphrase) To counter their unbelief He went about the villages teaching the people. What did He teach them, and how did He do it?

He did not make them sick, or punish them to try and teach them a lesson. Never! Instead He went about teaching the Word of God, replacing unbelief with faith. He healed everyone who had faith to believe Him and the word that He preached.

If God was ever going to teach people a lesson by making them sick, He would have done so to those people who rejected His Son. But He did not do that because He doesn't operate that way. Thank God for it!

Do not forget that John said in 1 John 3:8, **"For this purpose was the Son of God manifested, that** *he might destroy the works of the devil."* He did not come to do the devil's work, but rather destroy the devil's work. Jesus came to save humanity.

A moment to recap: God teaches by the written Word, and the Holy Spirit, and by the preached word, and by dealing with our hearts as is taught in I John 3:19-21, which reads as follows: *"And hereby we know that we are of the truth, and shall assure our hearts before him. For if our hearts condemn us, God is greater than our heart, and knoweth all things. Beloved, if our heart condemn us not, (then) have we confidence toward God."*

God has always dealt with man by speaking to his conscience, which is part of the spirit make-up of man. In the Book of Proverbs 20:27, it says that *"The spirit of man {is} the candle of the Lord, searching all the inward parts of the belly."* God is a Spirit, and He speaks to our spirit by illumination (revelation, inspiration). If, for some reason, God is unable to speak to us spiritually, He has no choice but to allow us the freedom to decide our course. And while we are going our own way death is at work. Proverbs 14:12, states, *"there is a way which seemeth right unto a man, but the end thereof {are} the ways of death."* Death is the end result of rebelling against God's laws. In Romans 6:23, Paul says, *"For the wages of sin {is} death; but the gift of God {is} eternal life through Jesus Christ our Lord."*

God has placed certain natural laws in the universe, and if we do not adhere to these we could be destroyed. For example, the law of gravity must not be abused by jumping from a building. If one jumps from a building without a net to catch him, he will become part of the concrete below.

Another thought: look at the natural laws of use (exercise) and health. If you bind your arm to your side so that it is immobilized for several months, and remove the binding, what would happen to your arm? Nothing. You could not use it because it had received no exercise. If our muscles aren't used we become weak and lifeless.

The law of use is important to the functioning and development of a normal, healthy body. Suppose you would never eat a properly balanced meal, but feasted only on sugar and water. It would not be long before you would die of malnutrition, or become diabetic. Our bodies have to have calcium for the bones, protein for strength and energy, and vitamins and so forth. Without vitamins and minerals we cannot survive very long. It is like trying to run an automobile without gas and oil. It will not work.

The same is true with regard to our relationship with God. We were designed spiritually to operate with God's Spirit and direction. If we forsake God, we cannot survive very long. We need God's word on a daily basis in order for us to function properly. In Proverbs 4:20-22, the word of God is health to our flesh. If you and I do not get a balanced diet of God's word in our heart, our souls and bodies will malfunction and eventually die.

God said, ***"My people are destroyed for a lack of knowledge".*** It is true, we will be destroyed by the devil, and sickness, and so many other things, simply because we refuse to heed God's word. And Paul writes, Romans 10:17, ***"So then faith {cometh} by hearing, and hearing by the word of God."*** If you want faith to resist the thief who comes to steal your health, you will have to keep taking God's word as a medicine.

We can only resist the devil by faith, as I Peter 5:9, Ephesians 6:16, and James 4:17 reveals to us. Please do not misunderstand what I am trying to say. Even as Christians, unless God would do something extremely out of the ordinary, we will die whether we hear the word of God or not.

But what I am saying is that we greatly increase the risk of dying before our time by rejecting God's Word. Reading God's Word, and obeying it, is the key to a successful life now and hereafter.

Allow God to lead and teach you by His Word and Spirit, and receive your healing and health. If you were trapped by this false idea that sickness or tragedy was meant to teach you something, then please ask God to forgive you, and pray this out loud, *"Dear Lord Jesus, I thank You for Your 'words of life.' I did not realize that You were not trying to teach me a lesson by this sickness or disease, but You have always wanted to lead me because You are the Good Shepherd. Please forgive me for not understanding You or Your Word. I receive Your forgiveness by faith, and I also receive Your guidance by the Holy Spirit. Now, I realize that You did not cause this to happen to me, and I am looking to You Father, for deliverance in this matter, In Jesus Name."*

Turn to chapter 20, and continue with your healing,

74

in Jesus name. Should you still have a problem, and you feel as though there is still something blocking your healing, please continue to the next page. God is looking forward to meeting your every need, and give you the Kingdom, Luke 12: 31-32, *"**But rather seek ye the kingdom of God; and all these things shall be added unto you. Fear not, little flock; for it is your Father's good pleasure to give you the kingdom.**"*

SECTION II

FOUR GREAT HINDRANCES TO RECEIVING HEALING

CHAPTER SIXTEEN

First, Unbelief

Unbelief is disbelief, faithlessness, also unfaithfulness coupled with disobedience.

I have covered unbelief just briefly in certain preceding passages, but I want to pursue it a little further. Unbelief is simply rejecting what God says is and can be.

Naturally, I am speaking of spiritual unbelief. We could possibly fail to believe in a certain person or thing, which would be considered as natural unbelief. But spiritually speaking, unbelief is rejecting the Word of God, and the Holy Spirit's working in one's life.

In religious circles, a sinner is normally considered as one who has not been born again or is unsaved. A sinner practices sin. A Christian would then be considered as one who practices the teachings of Christ. He is a follower of Christ, and is considered to be a believer.

Unbelievers could be considered those people who practice disbelief. They do not believe in the Word of God, or they may not believe in miracles or healing. If anyone believes the Bible to be the Living Word of God, they must also believe in miracles for today.

Unbelievers practice one of two things, or both: unbelief in God, and/or unbelief in God's Word. With their mouth they may profess to be believers, but they do not practice believing. For example, an unbeliever says that I am a Christian, and I believe that Jesus Christ is the same yesterday, today and forever. Yet, they do not live a life of faith. How sad is that?

You may ask some if they "believe that God will do the same today as He did in the days of the early church?" The unbeliever may say, *"No, God does not do that today."* You ask, *"When did God change?"* If the Lord saved and healed yesterday, He is obligated to do so today. Or, if not, He has changed His mind about humanity. He can't change because love is a constant. Either God will be a merciful God and faithful to a thousand generations, or He will not. (Deuteronomy 7:9). He said in Malachi 3:6, ***"For I {am} the Lord, I change not...,"***. He must love us all equally, or not love us at all. He has not changed. I believe He will always love us. He will always care for us, and our health. 3 John: 2.

Under the Old Testament, or Covenant, God took sickness away from the midst of the people, Exodus

22:25. Again in Psalms 103:2-3, there are two revelations of the benefits or blessings, under the Old Covenant, which were (1) He would forgive all their iniquities, and (2) He would heal all their diseases. Wonderful!

The New Testament, according to Hebrews 8:6, is *"a better covenant, which was established upon better promises."* In the New Covenant not only can we be healed but be saved eternally, and receive a glorified body after this life. The body will be like Jesus' body that will never die. I have not received my glorified body, yet, but some day, when Jesus returns for His church, I will receive one.

If you are saved when He returns, you will also receive a glorified body. But, until He returns, we have His promises of healing for our bodies which is made available through faith.

In This book, Chapters 20 & 21, I will be discussing the different "gifts of healing" which has been provided for the church and how to receive from God. Do not let unbelief keep you from receiving what God wants you to have, and the privileges that Jesus paid for. *"All things are possible to him that believeth,"* Mark 9:23. Be a believer!

Ask God to forgive you of any and all unbelief which has brought a snare upon you. Pray this out loud. Declare it with your mouth, and plead the blood of Jesus. It does not matter what people say or what they think, your health is what is important. You make a better witness when you can testify to the healing virtue of Jesus, and how Jesus lifted you up. Practice believing, and get well in Jesus name.

CHAPTER SEVENTEEN

Second, Words Of Our Mouth

In Proverbs 18:21 it declares, ***"Death and life {are} in the power of the tongue."***
Your health will depend a lot upon what you believe in your heart and speak with your mouth.

Also, in Proverbs 21:23, ***"Whoso keepeth his mouth and his tongue keepeth his soul from troubles."*** One of the reasons for our difficulties is the way we talk.

In Mark 7:18-23, Jesus taught that the things which we speak out of our hearts are things that defile us. And, James 3:1-12, is a discourse on the evils of the tongue. He said, ***"the tongue is a fire, a world of iniquity: so is the tongue among our members, that it defileth the whole body, and setteth on fire the course of nature; and is set*** *on fire of hell."* James went on to say that it is *"full of deadly poison."*

"A merry heart doeth good like a medicine: but a broken spirit drieth the bones," the Book of Proverbs 17:22. Our hearts are either filled with good or evil, and whatever is in the heart will be spoken from the mouth. With our tongues we either speak good or bad, and whatsoever we speak either gives us life, or works death.

There is awesome power in the tongue of man. So awesome in fact, that in Matthew 12:36-37, Jesus said that we would have to *"give account thereof in the day of judgment."* What words do you speak out of your mouth? Are they words that are wholesome, or damaging? Do you speak good things, or bad things?

In Mark 11:23, Jesus said, *"but shall believe that those things which he saith shall come to pass; he shall have whatsoever he saith."* If you believe in your heart that everything will turn out bad, and speak it with your mouth it will probably turn out bad.

So, start believing the good, speak it with your mouth, and you will receive it. But if your words are negative, then somewhere, at some point, the attitude of your heart must change, and you must begin speaking the good and positive with your mouth. Believe God's Word to be triumphant over everything. It is!!!

I remember a precious saint of God, who several years ago related to me the history of her arthritis. She said her leg was broken in an automobile accident, and as soon as it had happened, she said these words: *"You know, arthritis will set up in this leg when I get older."* And it did, just as she had believed and had spoken. She believed that in her heart, and she naturally spoke out what she believed.

If you find yourself thinking certain negative things, just do not speak them out. Replace bad thoughts with good ones. The Bible is the best source for "good thoughts." Speaking forth evil with your tongue is the same as acting out evil. Evil is not evil until you carry it out or speak it out.

Look at what Jesus said about the heart: If we **"look upon a woman with lust in our heart, it is adultery."** Matthew 5:28 The thought of a woman is not necessarily wrong, but it becomes sin when we make plans on how to put those thoughts into action. Keep your thoughts and hearts clean.

Watch your heart and keep your mouth or this may be your big down-fall. If you have spoken and thought only the bad and the negative, ask God to forgive you, right now. Ask Him to wash you in the blood of Jesus, and you confess your sin and He will forgive it. He will, if you will.

Have you slandered others with your mouth? What about your own family, spouse, children, etc.? Ask for forgiveness. The risks are too high, your health and life are at stake.

CHAPTER EIGHTEEN

Third, Unforgiveness

The third, and certainly not the least hindrance to receiving our healing, is not to forgive. So many people are plagued with infirmities, maladies, and other problems because of an unforgiving heart.

In many instances, during His earthly teachings, Jesus spoke of Unforgiveness. One such instance is shown in Mark 11:22-26, where Jesus taught on prayer, and receiving what we pray for. He coupled what we desire with praying, and the necessity of forgiving others who have wronged us. You may feel justified in your attitude over how others may have mistreated you, but you are without excuse before God where unforgiveness is concerned.

Even when we are innocent, or guilty, we have to forgive those who have trespassed against us. We are commanded to love everyone including our enemies. And we cannot love if we allow unforgiveness to stand between us. If you have ought in your heart against another, get it out. Repent, and ask God to forgive you for holding bitterness in your heart.

Perhaps you have thoughts of, *"I cannot forgive and forget what others have done,"* and these have been your constant companion. You can forgive! Do not listen to those negative thoughts. *"But how?"* you may ask. Answer: start by asking God to forgive you for any grudge or unforgiveness.

Second, say it out of your mouth. Pray this way; *"Lord Jesus, please forgive me for this unforgiveness, which I have kept in my heart against (their name). I forgive them as You forgive me. Help me every day Lord Jesus to speak forgiveness from my heart and mouth, In Your Name."*

It may be hard at first, but every day continue to pray in that fashion. Speak forth your forgiveness, even if that person never repents. Speak it forth; believing it with your heart, until it becomes easy and you know you are free.

Ask God to help you with it, and He will make a way. Before long you may be confronted by that same person, and you will know whether you have the victory over that unforgiveness. Practice forgiveness, in prayer, at the start of each day. You will succeed, according to Philippians 4:13, ***"I can do all things through Christ who strengthens me."***

CHAPTER NINETEEN

Fourth, Fear

Fear always goes hand-in-hand with unbelief; they are bosom buddies. But, rather than combining fear and unbelief into a single chapter, I thought that dealing with each as a separate issue would be to our advantage.

Fear is a spirit according to II Timothy1:7; and God is not the author of it. It is identified in Webster's New World Dictionary as (1.) a feeling of anxiety, an agitation caused by the presence or nearness of danger, evil, pain, etc.; timidity; dread; terror; fright; apprehension. (2.) awe, reverence, etc.

In the King James Version of the Bible, fear, and all of its root words, is used over four hundred and seventy (470) times. The following is a list of fourteen kinds of fear as mentioned in the scriptures, all of which God will deliver from, at our asking.

Hebrews 13:6, Fear of man.

Matthew 14:26, Fear of ghosts.

2 Timothy 1:7, A spirit of fear.

Psalms 23:4, Fear of evil.

Exodus 14:13, Danger.

Psalms 53:5, Imagined fear; nothing.

Job 4:14-16, Dreams.

Song of Solomon 3:8, Darkness.

Genesis 46:3, The future.

Judges 6:10, Idol gods.

Psalms 27:3, War.

Hebrews 2:15, Death.

Psalms 118: 3, Enemies.

Proverbs 1:26-27, Punishment.

Fear, when it takes hold, has the ability to paralyze or immobilize a person from action. Many sicknesses and diseases are attributed to or rooted in fear in the mind. These diseases are called psychosomatic because they originate in, or as a result of emotional distress, which may be from fear, anger, depression, etc. But fear is the one we want to zero in on.

The fear which causes us to cower; cringe; and withdraw is not of God. It is of the devil. It is a spirit which robs us of joy, relationships, creativity, optimism, hope, faith, expectancy, etc., and leaves us filled with dread, panic, alarm, terror, depression, rejection, insult, injury, and sickness.

The fear of cancer has probably caused more people to die prematurely, than all other diseases combined. People are terrified of this disease. When it attaches itself to their bodies, many just give up hope. It seems to be the last straw which breaks the proverbial donkey's back.

Cancer is a terrible disease, and has to be one of the most horrible nightmares created by the devil. But thanks be unto God for the victory which was won by Jesus Christ. He defeated the devil and all diseases "hands down", so to speak.

Our victory is in Jesus Christ our Lord. All Diseases, including cancer, does not stand a chance when we turn it over to Jesus. Like all spirits, fear has to present itself to us. If we receive that spirit, it will cause us to become fearful and turn inward.

Fear should never be resident in a person, but it stands without and makes fearful suggestions to that person. If a door is opened to fear it will come in, and afterwards it causes a person to take on the nature of fear, and react accordingly.

Sometime in the fall of 1977, while heading toward Bristol, Virginia, I knew I was going to be late for an appointment. Due to road repairs, heavy traffic, trying to make up time, and so forth, I had become too careless. As I was approaching an intersection, and hoping to beat the next light change, I had drifted too close to the vehicle in front of me. All of a sudden the driver in front of me slammed on his brakes, and I knew that stopping in time to prevent a terrible accident was impossible.

As I hit my brakes, I cried out, *"Jesus!"* then I hit him in the rear end. The impact was so hard that I knew that both cars had suffered severe damage. Fear presented itself to me. I fought back. I said, *"No, I will not respond to and by fear. I refuse to fear, In Jesus Name."* Fear left as quickly as it had come.

After determining that my family was OK, I jumped from my vehicle to see the extent of the damage to both vehicles. As I met the other driver, I asked how he and his passengers were doing. He said everyone was fine, no one was hurt. To our amazement there was not any damage to either vehicle. We searched for even a scratch, but there was none. The license plate on my front bumper was slightly bent, which was the only evidence of an accident.

I had learned two unforgettable lessons from this experience, which helped to change me for the good: One, I had learned that during emergencies, or very hazardous situations, by speaking only the name of Jesus protection is available. How wonderful it is to have a Savior who is a *"very present help in the time of trouble."* His "*name is above every name*!" Two, I understand that fear really is a spirit, and that people do not have to obey it. Fear can be refused just as we can refuse the spirit of murder, adultery, theft, and lying. We do not have to be motivated by fear.

If you have been tormented by fear, worry, alarm, panic, and anxieties, do you desire to be free? In I John 4:18, it says, ***"There is no fear in love; but perfect love casteth out fear: because fear hath torment. He that feareth is not made perfect in love."***

Have you been afraid? Then turn to God with your whole heart. Be free in Jesus name. Pray the following words with your mouth, and let love drive out fear. *"Dear Lord Jesus, I now realize that fear is not from You. Fear is a spirit sent from the enemy to steal my faith and joy. Please forgive me, Lord, for listening to the lies of the enemy. I, right now, resist the spirit of fear. I will not be afraid." "Fill me, Lord, with Your presence and love. Your love will cast out all fear. Fear, leave me now, in Jesus Name." "Thank You Jesus, for setting me free and for filling me with Your love."*

After you have removed all the mental and spiritual blocks from your spirit and mind, proceed to Section III, and be well in Jesus name.

SECTION III
HEALING MADE AVAILABLE

CHAPTER TWENTY

Avenues of Healing

God has chosen many avenues of healing. The following is a list of those known by this author, and those mentioned in the Bible.

A. Natural Healing

B. Doctors and Medicines

C. Asking and Receiving

D. Gifts of the Holy Spirit

E. Anointing with Oil and Prayers of the Elders

I feel it is necessary to look at all the types of healing which have been made available to the human race. However, because I am not a medical doctor, my comments about Natural Healing, Doctors and Medicines will be brief. A doctor should be consulted for further questioning concerning these subjects.

A. Natural Healing

Natural healing is a term I have chosen to refer to the wonderful way which God has made the human body. In Psalms 139:14, David says, ***"For I am fearfully and wonderfully made."***

Within all human beings, God has designed a means of self- healing. For instance, if we break a bone, and it is properly set in place, the body will begin to mend itself. The bone will become whole again as calcium is deposited over the break, and experience teaches that the bone will be stronger than before, in that area.

What about a cut, laceration, puncture, burn, or an abrasion? Normally, a cut or such will heal itself over a period of time, barring any extenuating circumstances where there has been severe tissue and/or nerve damage, which would prevent natural healing. Even those may heal in time.

Built into our systems is a natural fortress for fighting off diseases. This fortress is called the "Natural Immunity System." (my words) The body was designed with this natural immunity to repel bacteria which may be harmful to the body. For instance, when an infection or germ invades the body, special cells and substances called antibodies (found in the blood) destroys the invaders. White blood cells are our soldiers on guard, standing ready to attack any foreign object which may enter our bodies.

However, there are people who have problems where the white blood cells simply cannot fight off an attack. These people must be helped by medicine or some alternate source.

AIDS (Acquired Immunity Deficiency Syndrome) or the effect of it seems to be the complete loss of the ability to fight certain kinds of infection. People who have AIDS are very susceptible to a rare cancer and brain damage, and destruction of the nervous system. All of the effects of AIDS are certainly not known.

Unless a person has some problem with their immune system, or it is weak, healing is normally built into the body to keep it well. Much more could be said, but I dare not say more for the lack of space and time, and professional knowledge. But I thank God for his marvelous design of the natural healing for the human body.

B. Doctors and Medicines

Thank God for good doctors, nurses and medicines. Many doctors and scientists have spent their lifetime in search of cures or helps for ailing humanity. Some examples: Doctor Jonas Salk worked from twelve to fourteen hours a day, but it took years to develop the vaccine which all but wiped out polio. And Doctor Louis Pasteur, who is noted for his rabies treatment and pasteurization; Florence Nightingale was the epitome of what a nurse could and should be. Doctor Albert Schweitzer, medical missionary to Africa, and Mark Buntain to India, are men who gave all in service for God and man, and should not be forgotten because of their contributions to health and healing. If listed, those who have worked so hard and given so much to help the afflicted and diseased would be almost endless.

Healing is from God. Whether we receive it by laying on of hands, or doctors and medicines. As in any profession, many doctors are in it for the name and money. These will abort babies and destroy without even a flinch, or blinking of an eye. The "Oath of Service" taken at ordination means nothing to them. Life means nothing to them. But thank God for those who practice with a heart to serve others.

Like doctors, medicines have come a long way. Many people have been spared because they received help from a known medicine. And many of these would have died lost without Christ, but were given an extension on life by medicine, and later sought God's forgiveness.

This is really true in many third-world countries where medical help is virtually non-existent. Because of those like Doctor Schweitzer, many people have received Jesus Christ as Lord and Savior because they were first helped medically. When people see that you love them and are trying to help them, it is much easier to preach Jesus to them.

As stated in Chapter 2, *"God will use doctors and medicines,"* but an instantaneous healing is better by far. Having God perform surgery without a knife is much easier. Amen?

C. Asking and receiving

We need to always be thankful for our Heavenly Father, for Jesus said, ***"that whatsoever ye shall*** *ask of the Father in my name, He may give it you.*" (John 15:16)

In Matthew 15:21-28, is related the incident of a heathen woman asking for Jesus to cast a demon out of her daughter. At first, Jesus ignored her, but she kept crying out, *"O Lord, thou Son of David; my daughter is grievously vexed with a devil."* In verse 25, she came and worshipped him, saying, "Lord, help me," in so many words.

Even when it seemed that Jesus ignored her, implying that she was a dog, she was still persistent. She kept on asking, and got what she wanted. She was determined.

Remember Luke 18:1, we are to *"pray and not faint"*. Also, in Matthew, 7: 7-11, we are told to *"ask, seek, & knock."* Keep on asking. Keep on seeking. Keep on knocking. Those who do these things will receive. If you mean business with God, then don't give up. You will be rewarded.

After you begin asking God for healing, or whatever, listen closely to your heart. God will begin to put a desire into your heart about how to receive your healing. He will tell you what to do to receive, or He may just do an instantaneous miracle, right then, with no one around.

He may confirm His actions with a scripture reference. However He (God) decides to handle your situation, it is up to Him and you. But, whatever, He will let you know, and you will know. This knowing will be the gift of faith in operation, and it will produce the desired results if you hold fast to it.

Most Important! Do not stop asking, seeking, praising and being thankful. If you listen to the Holy Spirit, Who is speaking to your heart, He will probably use one of the avenues of the "gifts of healing," to minister to you. This will be a supernatural enablement working to heal through an individual. Whatever method that God uses to heal you it will be according to your faith.

Read through the four Gospels and Acts of the Apostles and notice the many ways that people were healed and delivered.

D. Gifts of the Holy Spirit

In I Corinthians 12:1-11, Paul was instructed to write to the church in Corinth and explain the different gifts of the Holy Spirit. These gifts are not resident in people, but will go into operation at the discretion of the Holy Spirit, and where faith is in action on the part of the one who needs a healing. These gifts are for ministering where there is a need: in order to build-up the church and meet the needs of humanity.

Since we are talking about healing, my emphasis will be about the same. All of these gifts will operate in the lives of believers.

(1.) Word Of Wisdom

God may tell you where to go, or what to do, to receive your healing, or help. This would be a Word of Wisdom. Do whatever God says, and be blessed. He may give this Word personally or through anyone in the church who believes.

(2.) Word of Knowledge

God may reveal to one a "Word of Knowledge," telling them a person has a certain disease, or affliction, and that He is going to heal them. If that person believes, and they believe it without doubting, God will perform His word.

A "Word of Knowledge" may be so detailed as to give name, address, problem, and date when the healing will take place. A "Word of Knowledge" from God builds our faith to the place that we can receive a miracle from Him.

(3.) Gifts of Faith

There may be the time when the "Gift of Faith" may go into operation in your own life or someone else. This gift of faith will drive out all doubt and unbelief, leaving you with the knowing that all is well. Faith may become so strong that you may be as Peter was and walk on the water. Or, the Hebrew Children going into the midst of the fiery furnace. This supernatural faith will move any mountain in your life. Like all the gifts, ask for it. Desire it!

(4.) Gifts of Healing

In I Corinthians 12:28, It is called Gifts of Healing, meaning many, or varied means of healing. Here are a few examples of healing or deliverance, as recorded in the Bible.

1. Mark 16:18, Luke 13:13, Mark, 6:5, James 5:14,15, Laying on of hands by the elders and believers.

2. James 5:14-15, Mark 6:13, Anointing with all in Jesus' Name and prayer.

3. James 5:14-16, Prayers of faith by believers.

4. Acts 19:12, Prayer cloths received by believers for others.

5. John 9:6, Mark 7:32, 33, Spit, or spit and clay by a believer.

6. II Kings 5, John 9:7, Dipping in water, or washing in a pool.

7. Luke 7:1-10, Acts 3:1-10, Acts 16:18, Acts 14:9,10, A command of faith given by a believer.

8. Matthew 18:18-19, Acts 12:5, Standing in agreement by two or more believers.

I am sure that you may find in the Bible many other ways which God has chosen to perform a miracle. But here is something significant about each incident where a miracle was performed. In each situation someone (or group) had to believe by faith, and do something to demonstrate their faith.

In order to receive a miracle we must act upon God's word, or His command.

Examples:

Enoch walked with God, Who was pleased with him and translated him to heaven. Faith pleases God.

*Noah believed God, built an Ark and was delivered from the flood. He began the ark by faith, first.

*Abraham believed God and received the great promise even in his old age.

*Samson believed God, kept his vows, and had supernatural strength.

*David looked to God, ran to meet the giant, and dropped him with a stone.

*Elijah built an altar and put his offering on it, before he prayed and God sent the fire.

*In Joshua's day, the priests had to step into the flooding water before God held back the water. They moved by faith.

*Naaman had to dip seven times before the leprosy was cured.

*The Hebrew boys declared their faith in God before being thrown into the flames, and they did not burn.

*Jesus told Peter to come, and Peter by faith got out of the boat and walked on the water.

*Jesus told the blind man to go wash. He did, and his eyes were opened. True faith always receives for what it is believing. He obeyed before he saw.

The woman said beforehand, "If I touch his garment, I will be healed." She did. She was healed. She saw herself healed through the eyes of faith because she believed Jesus had the power and the willingness to heal her.

Elisha threw the meal into the pot before the poison was neutralized.

The people had to fill the water pots first before Jesus would turn the water to wine.

Moses had to hit the rock before the water came out.

Moses had to throw the staff on the ground before it would become a serpent. He had to grab the serpent by the tail before it would turn back to a staff.

Moses threw ashes into the air before the boils came upon the Egyptians.

Moses had to stretch forth his hand before the hail came.

Moses had to smite the dust with his staff before it turned to lice.

Jesus began to minister the bread before it was multiplied and over 5,000 were fed, in one instance.

Do you get the picture? Faith demands action; Faith first, results second! Even when you don't see how it could possibly work, begin by faith.

If someone lays hands on you, and anoints you with oil, or whatever, and you sense in your heart *"that it is God"*, then receive by faith. No matter how foolish it seems, do it. After prayer, or a direct word from God, act as though it is fixed and it will be fixed.

Gifts of Healing may operate through many different channels. A word, a command to "be healed" or "be whole", an anointed cloth, a prayer of agreement, laying on of hands, and even a clay poultice made from spittle may be some avenues which God may use to minister to you.

Never be close-minded toward even the foolish methods which God may use to get healing to you.

(5.) Working of Miracles

A healing is getting well, or recovering; whereas a miracle is a creative, supernatural work of God. A person is healed of cancer or leprosy through gifts of healing or prayer of faith, anointing with oil, etc., but if a person is blind, or doesn't have an eyeball, a miracle is needed for that person to see. An eye would have to be created.

Jesus turned the water to wine. The gift of healing wasn't used, but a working of miracles by the Holy Spirit was required to chemically change water to wine.

If there is sickness or disease, a healing is necessary. If something is damaged, or missing, then a miracle is required to restore to the normal condition.

Knowing the difference when you pray is important.

Because when you ask God to heal you, ask for a healing. If you are damaged or something has been destroyed, then you need to believe and ask for a miracle.

If it is a case of needing finances, or casting out an unclean spirit, faith is what is needed. Ask God for what you need, and expect the Holy Spirit to increase your faith with supernatural faith. And by all means, get into the word of God.

Suppose that an unclean spirit is at work and you have the symptoms of cancer. The doctors may even diagnose your problem as cancer. Yet, the Holy Spirit may begin to operate the gift of discerning (distinguishing) of spirits through someone and they would declare this to be a work of an unclean spirit. At which time, the unclean spirit would have to be cast out of the body, in Jesus' name.

After an unclean spirit has been cast out, and there is still evidence of a sickness or disease, then ask God for a healing. Many times when an unclean spirit has been exorcised, even the symptoms of diseases will leave an individual.

6.) Other Gifts of the Spirit

Like all the gifts of the Holy Spirit, prophecy, different kinds of tongues, and interpretation of tongues are used to edify and exhort the body of Christ. God may use these gifts to help break the power of disease and/or even unclean spirits from the lives of people.

God will work through whatever faith we have to

offer Him. So, have great faith in God, knowing that He loves you with an unfailing love.

Anointing with Oil and Prayer of the Elders

"Is anyone sick? He should call for the elders for the church and they should pray over him, and pour a little oil upon him, calling on the Lord to heal him. And their prayers, if offered in faith, will heal him, for the Lord will make him well; and if his sickness was caused by some sin, the Lord will forgive him." James 5:14,15, The Book; Living Bible.

The elders are the church leaders, or spiritual overseers, who are qualified for their positions by the Holy Spirit. These elders meet the qualifications of I Timothy 3, and Titus 1:5-9, and they have the authority of binding and loosing, as recorded in Matthew 18:18.

The oil represents the Holy Ghost. As the elders of the church, working in agreement with the Holy Spirit (Lord in the church), and anoint with oil (symbol of the Holy Spirit), the power and authority of heaven and earth are set in motion to bring about healing and forgiveness. It is almost as if the oil represents the badge of authority or symbol of agreement.

As long as there are elders in the church, the Holy Spirit will not override their authority, but will work with their authority. The power and authority of running the church affairs was given to the elders by Jesus Christ. The decisions, directions, and wisdom for administering the affairs of church government were to come from the wisdom of the teaching of the

Holy Spirit.

In Acts, Chapter 15, is a prime example of the church leaders working with the Holy Spirit. In verses 4,6 the apostles and elders came together to consider a matter. In verse 28, James says in a letter to some Jewish Christians; *"for it seemed good to the Holy Ghost, and to us.."*

The apostles and elders were not sure how that situation was to be handled, but the Holy Spirit gave the solution. They acted upon the Holy Spirit's wisdom, and gave their advice and decision, accordingly.

The Holy Spirit will not force his wisdom on pastors, teachers, elders, etc., but works through their willingness to be led as sons of God. The Holy Ghost leads, and the elders carry out the wishes of Jesus Christ in the church.

Some may contend that elders are no longer in the church, but that is not so. As long as there is a church there will be overseers of that church. But, elders have to be believers, Mark 16:17-18.

As the elders came together in agreement (Matthew 18:18-20), anointing with the oil (sign of the Holy Spirit's authority and presence), they prayed the prayer of faith, and sickness and diseases were driven out. And where there had been sin, it was forgiven.

I also believe that where demons have held authority through sin, the power of sin will be broken, and the demons driven away. For whatever is *"bound on earth, will be bound in heaven; and whatever*

is loosed on earth, will be loosed in heaven. "
Amen!

This avenue for healing is sure and absolute, even for those with little faith. Act upon God's word, which cannot fail.

CHAPTER TWENTY-ONE

Let's Get Well, In Jesus Name

Up to this point and time, we have discussed:

(1) Teachings which may have mentally blocked our healing;

(2) Spiritual blocks which may have hindered our healing;

(3) Avenues for healing.

We have determined according to scripture that it is God's will to heal us, supernaturally, by His power. Or, He may use doctors and medicines for our healing, and that's according to our faith.

After you have prayed and removed all hindrances blocking you spiritually and mentally, it is time to seek God for your healing. Begin by following these simple steps:

1. Enter into His presence by thanksgiving and praise, Psalms 100:4; I Thessalonians 5: 18. Thank Him for who He is. He is your healer, and He is and has everything that you need, Exodus 15:26. Thank Him for the privilege of prayer and asking, John 14:14, Matthew 7:7, Jeremiah 29:12-13. Thank Him for the Blood of Jesus, Romans 5:9, Hebrews 10:19, Colossians 1:20. Thank Him that healing has been provided through the atoning sacrifice of Jesus Christ, Isaiah 53:5; Matthew 8:17; I Peter 2:24. Thank Him for hearing your prayers, Psalms 34:10; Psalms 103:1-3; Matthew 6:33; Matthew 7:7-8; Jeremiah 29:12-13; Psalms 34:6; Matthew 14:14-15; James 5:14-15.

2. Make your request known to God, Philippians 4:6-7. Allow the Holy Spirit to pray through you, Romans 8:26-27; I Corinthians 14:14-15; Jude 20. When asking, be specific, tell Him what you want.

3. Listen to the Holy Spirit's direction and leading, Romans 8:14; John 16:13-14. The Spirit of God will guide you, according to your faith, to your point of healing, John 16:13. The Holy Spirit will take you through each step so that you may receive your healing, Psalms 37:23; Psalms 121:1-3; Psalms 84:11.

4. Exercise your faith, i.e., use your faith. If the Spirit of God has spoken to your heart to do something, do it! Obey the Holy Spirit and take that step of faith. Should you sense in your heart that you need to call the elders of the church to anoint you with oil and pray for you, do it. Trust God's word and act upon it.

Should you feel to attend an evangelistic meeting where they believe in praying for the sick, then go in faith that you will receive your healing.

Some ministers may speak over the radio, television, or in person, and a "Word of Knowledge" may be spoken which describes your situation. If so, accept it by faith as a word from God, and be healed.

You may be sitting at home, driving in a car, or taking a shower, and God may speak a word to your heart. He may say, *"You will recover."* Should that happen, thank Him by faith, and do not doubt.

Faint not, doubt not; persevere with faith. Be as tenacious as the Canaanite woman about her daughter, Matthew 15:21-28. Remember, God wants to heal you, and He is taking the necessary steps that it will take to get you delivered. He is constantly working on your faith. If God said that He would do what we ask of Him, then He will do it. Anything which brings doubt is not of God.

5. Pray the scriptures when you pray. Quote the scriptures as you pray and this will keep you in the will of God, I John 5: 14-15. Lean not to your own understanding as you pray, as you work, on a daily basis; Proverbs 3:5-6. God watches over His word to perform it, Jeremiah 1:12.

He will cause His word to prosper, Isaiah 55:11.

He upholds all things by His word, Hebrews 1:3. Heaven and Earth will pass away before God will let His word fail, Matthew 24:35.

Jesus said, *"Therefore I say unto you, What things so ever ye desire, when you pray believe that you receive them and ye shall have them."* Mark 11:24.

Whatsoever ye desire, pray, believe and receive. How simple to receive from God. If we could see how much that God loves us; to give us whatsoever we desire.

6. Changing life styles. Because God loves us so much He will always have our best interest at heart. If our life style was the reason that we became ill, God may choose not to heal us until we make some changes.

Example: If you were a heavy smoker most of your life, and later on you discovered that you had developed lung cancer; God may say to you, *"Stop smoking and I will heal you."*

Example: A homosexual contracts the AIDS virus. God says, *"Before I heal you, you will have to repent of your life style."*

Example: A man may have a reproductive disorder. He asks God to heal him of that problem, but God says, *"You have been living in adultery: you repent, and I will heal you."*

We could use an example of a liver disorder by an alcoholic, or an eye problem of a porno addict. However, God may choose to heal all of these people even before they repent, but one thing is for sure, He expects them to make some changes in the way they live.

In John 8, the adulteress woman escaped certain

death because of Jesus' compassion. When the religious people wanted her to be stoned, Jesus temporarily got her off the hook. But in verse 11, He told her, *"Neither do I condemn thee; go, and sin no more."* Go, and do not practice adultery anymore.

The same was true in John 5:14, when Jesus told the man to *"sin no more, lest a worse thing come unto thee."* God will not always do these good things for us just so we can continue living in rebellion against Him.

God wants all of us to be in health, and to be prosperous, and live a full and productive life. But the only way to live a full and productive life is to allow Jesus to be our Shepherd and Lord, Psalms 23:1; John 14:6.

We must learn to trust Him, Psalms 37:3; Proverbs 3:6-7. Because He is a "Good Parent," *"No good thing will He withhold from those that walk uprightly,"* Psalms 84: 11. *"Every good gift... is from the Father"*, James 1:18. He gives good gifts, Matthew 7:11. God wants us to be in *"health, as our soul prospers"*, III John 2.

7. Persevere With Praise *"Offer unto God thanksgiving; and pay they vows unto the Most High: and call upon me in the day of trouble: I will deliver thee, and thou shalt glorify me,"* Psalms 50: 14-15.

Healing brings God glory, Matthew 15:30-31. *"Who so offereth praise glorifieth me; and to him that ordereth his conversation aright* (way of

110

life) **will I show the salvation (deliverance) of God,"** Psalms 50:23.

God dwells in praise according to Psalms 22:3. Praise denotes the presence of God. And in Psalms 9:2-3, as we sing the praise of God, our enemies will fall back at the presence of the Most High. Praise God and watch your enemies of sickness and maladies begin to fall away.

Never complain, but rather live a life of praise before the Lord. Praise by faith: even when you hurt. When you have done all that you know to do, just stand; Resist the devil; praise God for His mercy. When temptations comes, and you feel like giving up or going under because you have not seen a change in your situation: hold onto God by faith, through praise.

God knows how to take you through the temptations of the devil, I Corinthians 10:13 and He knows how to deliver you from them, 2 Peter 2:9. **"I will call upon the Lord, who is worthy to be praised: so shall I be saved** (delivered) **from mine enemies,"** Psalms 18:3.

Death is an enemy, I Corinthians 15:26 and anything which causes death would be an enemy. **"By Him** (Jesus**) therefore let us offer the sacrifice of praise to God continually, that is the fruit of our lips, giving thanks to His name,"** Hebrews 13:15. Praise Him, continually.

As a pastor/evangelist, I have received many telephone calls from individuals asking for prayer. We would pray and stand in agreement, and at first there would not be any change, but, I would have the caller to start praising God for who He is. As this praise goes forth something seems to break, or almost snap, immediately. Especially, when we say things like, *"Thank You, Lord, for healing and nothing can stand in Your way Jesus when You begin to move."* Praise Him! Brag and Boast on Him! God is worthy of all our praise and adoration.

Healing is made available. That's God's responsibility. Believing is our opportunity to receive what is provided though the price that Jesus paid for our full redemption: spirit, soul, and body.

CHAPTER TWENTY-TWO

Staying Healed and Walking in Health

First, as long as we live in this body, on this earth, we will come under attack of the devil and his cohorts. The devil is an adversary, and he does not fight fair, I Peter 5: 8-9; John 8: 44; John 10:10; Ephesians 6:11.

He works through children of disobedience. Ephesians 2:2. He blinds people to the truth. II Corinthians 4:3-4. No wonder he is called a serpent and deceiver in Revelations 12:9.

It is spiritual suicide to:

*Ignore the reality of who our enemy is.

*Not put on the whole armor of God.

*Bury our heads in the "religious sand pile."

Second, Through Jesus Christ we have the victory. Praise God! The Victory over sin was won at Calvary. The victory over hell was won in hell by Jesus. The victory over death was won when Jesus was beaten with 39 stripes.

Jesus has the keys of death and hell, and *"I can do all things through Christ, who strengthens me"*. Philippians 4:13.

The enemy who first stole your health will come again. If he was able to hurt you before, then he will try to bring that sickness back to you. He must be resisted, in Jesus name. James 4:7; I Peter 5:8-9. Even though attacks will come, the greater one lives in us. If we want to walk in the victory, keep the sin out.

Tips For Victory

1. Why should we keep the sin out of our personal lives and business?

*Sin originates from and gives *"place to the devil"*. Ephesians 4:27.

**"He that committeth sin* (practices sin) *is of the devil."* I John 3:8.

**"If I regard iniquity in my heart the Lord will not hear me."* Psalms 66:18.

**"He that covereth his sin shall not prosper"*. Proverbs 28: 13.

**"And your sins have hid His face from you, that He will not hear."* Isaiah 59:2.

114

*Get the sin out. I John 1:8-9.

*God has **"no pleasure"** in those who **"draw back"** from Him. Hebrews 10:38-39.

***"The Lord's curse is on the house of the wicked, but He blesses the home of the righteous."** Proverbs 3:33, N.I.V.

2. Knowing God's Plans

God is His Word, and in His Word. John 1:1.

* The universe **"consists"** through Him. Colossians 1:17, that is, it stands because it stands through Him.

* **"He upholds all things by the Word of His Power."** Hebrews 1:3.

* His "**word is forever**" settled (established) in heaven, Psalms 119:09-91.

* He always "**watches over His word to perform it**", Jeremiah 1:12.

* So, the Psalmist said, **"Thy word have I hid in my heart, that I might not sin against thee."** Psalms 119:11. He understood the key to success was in obeying (keeping) the word of God.

  Many times we get into trouble because we do not know what the word of God says. In Hosea 4:6, the word says, **"My people are destroyed for a lack of knowledge."** We only hurt ourselves when we do not walk in God's word.

The word of God is *"life unto those who find them, and health to all their flesh,"* Proverbs 4:22.

3. We must continue in His word

Not only must we know God's word, but we have to be doers of the word. If the word of God is health to our flesh, then we must get the word into us on a daily basis.

If you have high-blood pressure and you are on a prescribed medication to keep it under control: a stroke could be in the making if you fail to follow up or continue with the medication.

The word of God must be acted upon daily before we reap the real benefits from it. Take heavy dosages of the Words of Life every day.

Be a doer of the word, continually, John 8:31-32; John 15:7; James 1:22-25; James 2:26; Colossians 2:7-8. Mediate on God's words, Proverbs 3:6-7; Psalms 1:1-3; Joshua 1:7-9.

4. Making Other Changes in Our Life Styles

As stated in Chapter 21, our life styles need to be changed. Sin has been discussed in several instances. What about gluttony? Is our problem one of overeating or not eating properly? Luke 21:34. We need to get a handle on our eating habits. Poor diets are a great attributive to many health problems. We ask God to heal us of many diseases, but are we willing to give up foods which are doing our bodies harm, I Corinthians 9:27; I Corinthians 6:12.

5. Let Love Be Your Constant Companion.

Continue in the love of Jesus, John 15:9; Hebrews 13:1.

Always treat others the way you would want to be treated, Matthew 7:12.

Be merciful, Matthew 5:7.

Give your love away to those who are in need, Isaiah 58:7-8; Luke 14:12-14.

Love will always continue, I Corinthians 13:13.

Have love over top of all, Colossians 3:14.

Keep yourselves in the love of God, Jude 21.

Minister health and healing to others in Jesus name, and God will minister health to you, Galatians 6:9-10.

CLOSING REMARKS

Dear Friends,

"I pray that you may enjoy good health and that all may go well with you, even as your soul is getting along well." III John 2, N.I.V.

Remember, *"Surely He hath borne our griefs and carried our sorrows: yet we did esteem Him stricken, smitten of God, and afflicted. But He was wounded for our transgressions, He was bruised for our iniquities: the chastisement of our peace was upon Him; and with His stripes we are healed."* Isaiah 53: 4-5. Jesus was the Servant Who received our just punishment, but did so that we could receive His life and that more abundantly. Always stay under the Blood of Jesus.

Your brother in Christ,

Darrell Davis

ABOUT THE AUTHOR

I, DARRELL DAVIS was born again September 18, 1974 after an encounter with an unexpected guest. On that evening, and after returning home from work as an assistant manager of a general- merchandise store, I decided to do what bachelors do: open cans of whatever could be found and throwing it on the stove. After setting the table for one, I sat down to eat, and I felt a holy presence enter the room. I knew from the time that I was a child that this presence was The Lord Jesus. Later, I knew it was The Holy Spirit on behalf of Jesus.

Immediately, I felt conviction because of my sins, and this is all I knew to pray, ***"God, forgive me of every sin that I have ever committed."*** Something happened inside of me: I knew He had forgiven me. I felt clean. The desire for the drugs, alcohol, rock N roll, and the old lifestyle was gone. And when I ran into some ole friends and thought it was necessary to lace my speech with a few "cuss" words, I felt horrible. I knew that I had offended the Holy Spirit. So, the "cussin'" had to go.

The call to preach: While attending an evangelistic meeting at a church near Grundy, VA, on a Wednesday night, there were two ladies whom I had never seen or met before that evening. Each in turn stepped behind me, lightly touching me on the head, and were speaking in languages which I had never heard before. But, I knew it to be a holy gesture from the mighty presence of God. I wept like a baby. I had never met the visiting evangelist, and he stood and interpreted what the two women had spoken in those languages.

"For thus saith the Lord, 'I have called you out of darkness to do a work for Me.'"

Within three months I began preaching in the local jail, and that ministry has continued into several states and penal institutions, and several nations. To God be the glory.

Darrell has two other books which he has authored and are available on Amazon.com

1. Letters To My Friends, Volume I

2. Letters To My Friends, Volume 2

$9.95 in paperback & $5.99 in Kindle Edition

"God Loves You More Than The devil Can Hate You!"